# THE SALEM WITCH TRIALS

## Mass Hysteria and Many Lives Lost

BY MICHAEL BURGAN

Consultant:
Richard Bell, PhD
Associate Professor of History
University of Maryland, College Park

**CAPSTONE PRESS**
a capstone imprint

Tangled History is published by Capstone Press,
1710 Roe Crest Drive, North Mankato, Minnesota 56003
www.mycapstone.com

Library of Congress Cataloging-in-Publication Data

Names: Burgan, Michael, author
Title: The Salem witch trials : mass hysteria and many lives lost / by
Michael Burgan.
Description: North Mankato, Minnesota : Capstone Press, 2019. |
Series: Tangled history | Includes bibliographical references and index.
Identifiers: LCCN 2018036899| ISBN 9781543541977 (hardcover) | ISBN
9781543542011 (pbk.) | ISBN 9781543542059 (ebook pdf)
Subjects: LCSH: Trials (Witchcraft)—Massachusetts—Salem—History—Juvenile
literature. | Witchcraft—Massachusetts—Salem—History—Juvenile literature. |
Salem (Mass.)—History—Colonial period, ca. 1600–1775—Juvenile literature.

Classification: LCC KFM2478.8.W5 B87 2019 | DDC 133.4/3097445--dc23

LC record available at https://lccn.loc.gov/2018036899

Editorial Credits
Michelle Bisson, editor; Tracy McCabe, designer; Svetlana Zhurkin, media
researcher; Laura Manthe, production specialist

Photo Credits
Alamy: Classic Image, 62, Lebrecht Music and Arts Photo Library, cover, The History
Collection, 10, 14; Bridgeman Images: Collection of the New-York Historical Society, USA/
Witch Hill (The Salem Martyr) 1869 (oil on canvas), Noble, Thomas Satterwhite (1835-
1907), 54, Look and Learn/Private Collection/On Trial, When Satan Came to Salem,
1978 (gouache on paper), English School, (20th century), 26, Look and Learn/Private
Collection/Salem Witch Trials (litho), English School, (20th century), 20–21; Getty Images:
DeAgostini, 69, Hulton Archive, 66; Granger, 45, 71; Newscom: Everett Collection, 37, 64,
Xinhua/Li Yan, 103; North Wind Picture Archives, 4, 7, 24, 52, 60, 76, 82–83, 88, 90, 100;
Shutterstock: Everett Historical, cover (background), 29, 40, 59, 96, Pierdelune, 104; XNR
Productions, 16

Printed and bound in the United States of America.
PA49

# TABLE OF CONTENTS

In the 1600s colonists were called to church services by a drummer.

# FOREWORD

Starting in the 1620s, thousands of English Protestants known as Puritans began arriving in Massachusetts. They started the Massachusetts Bay Colony so that they could worship as they chose. In England they had lacked that religious freedom. The first settlement in the colony was Salem.

By the late 1680s, Boston had become the colony's major city, but Salem was still an important settlement. Its residents mostly fished, farmed, and bought and sold goods with other colonies and settlements. The center of Salem, near the waterfront, was called Salem Town. The community of Salem Village was several miles away.

Each community had its own church. Religious beliefs were central to the Puritans' world. They strictly followed the teachings in the Bible. Every property owner had to pay taxes to support local churches, even those who were not members of a church. Everyone was also required to go to church. In the early days of Massachusetts Bay, some people who challenged the Puritans' religious beliefs were forced out of the colony.

Over time, some residents did not follow the strict religious beliefs of the first settlers. That sometimes created conflicts between members of the same church. Salem Village experienced this, as some members of its church refused to pay taxes to support their minister.

The Puritans of Massachusetts Bay had other challenges as well. In rural parts of New England, such as Maine, and in New York, settlers faced attacks from French soldiers allied with the Wabanaki Indians. Several families in and around Salem had lived in Maine or had relatives there, so they worried about the fighting there. Massachusetts sometimes sent soldiers to fight on the frontier.

In addition, starting around 1690, English settlers from Maine flocked to Salem and other nearby towns for safety.

Massachusetts Bay colonists had many challenges that did not involve religion.

The towns had to pay higher taxes to help take care of those people and to support the military, who were fighting the French and Indians.

Puritan ministers believed that all these troubles were a sign that God was angry with the colony. Puritans considered themselves saints doing God's work and believed God took a direct interest in their lives. They thought that if the people of Massachusetts Bay did not follow the Bible's teachings, God punished them.

Along with their belief in God, Puritans also thought that devils were a real force. Leading the many devils was Satan, according to Puritan teachings. They thought that, through his devils, Satan tried to convince Christians to reject God. He did this, in part, by giving some people magical powers over other humans if they helped him. The people who made this deal with Satan were witches. The residents of Salem believed witches existed and could cause great harm. Across the American colonies and in Europe, Christians believed witchcraft was a real threat. In the Massachusetts Bay colony, the death penalty was the punishment for anyone found guilty of being a witch.

At the beginning of 1692, the many problems in the colony and the fear of witchcraft seemed poised to come together. In a very short time, that proved to be true.

Samuel Parris

# THE FIRST
# TROUBLES

As the new year began, Samuel Parris felt troubled by many things. Since becoming the minister for the church in Salem Village in 1689, he had quarreled with some of its residents. He knew they were not eager to pay taxes for his salary. He had persuaded village leaders to give him the house where he now lived, and some residents had opposed that. Other members of the church did not like Parris's strict religious teachings.

Puritans did not automatically become members of the local church. Instead, they had to explain to the congregation how they had come to accept Jesus Christ into their lives. The congregation then decided whether they could join. Once people became members, they could take part in communion. Male members also voted on how the church was run. Some people in Salem wanted to make it easier for people to become members of the congregation, but Parris and residents who supported him wanted to keep the old rules in place. The divisions in the village over these issues were not new. Salem Village had already lost several other ministers in recent years because of such problems.

With all these issues swirling around him, Parris often reminded the congregation that Satan was always trying to destroy the Puritan faith. He taught that Satan counted on the help of wicked men and women.

Something more personal was also bothering Parris. Starting in the middle of January, he noticed that his 9-year-old daughter Betty was acting strangely. So was her 11-year-old cousin Abigail Williams, who lived with the Parris family. At times, Parris found the girls huddled under chairs and making noises that didn't sound like words.

Parris and his wife, Elizabeth, tried curing the girls with herbs and other natural medicines. They also prayed to God, asking for his help. But neither prayers nor herbs worked. Parris called in Dr. William Griggs, who told the minister, "The girls are under an evil hand." Neighbors had been saying the same thing. Parris knew what they meant—Satan had sent witches to torment his family.

## Tituba

Salem Village, Massachusetts
February 25, 1692

Tituba watched as Mr. and Mrs. Parris left home to attend a religious lecture in another town. Tituba and her husband, John Indian, were enslaved people kept by the Parris family. As she and John went about their chores, a neighbor named Mary Sibley came over.

"People say the girls have been attacked by a witch," Sibley said. "You should bake a witch cake to find out who it is." Tituba knew from

Tituba (right) was one of the first to be falsely accused of witchcraft.

her time in Barbados what a witch cake was. She asked the girls for some of their urine and mixed it with rye. Once the cake was done, she and John fed it to the family dog. When the dog ate the cake, the witch who caused the girls' suffering should feel pain too. The pain might lead the witch to reveal his or her identity. Nothing happened immediately after the dog ate the witch cake. They would just have to wait to see if something would soon happen.

## Abigail Williams

Salem Village, Massachusetts
February 26, 1692

Abigail knew that Tituba had baked a witch cake. And since then, she had felt worse than before. "It is Tituba," she cried out to her aunt and uncle, Mrs. and Mr. Parris. "I can see her!"

"But she is not here, Abigail," Mr. Parris said.

"I can see her specter, it's like a ghost," Abigail wailed. "She is coming for me!"

Abigail began to run around the room, yelling that Tituba was out to get her. At times she struggled to breathe, as if she were being choked. Betty suffered in the same way. Mr. and Mrs. Parris looked panicked as they watched helplessly.

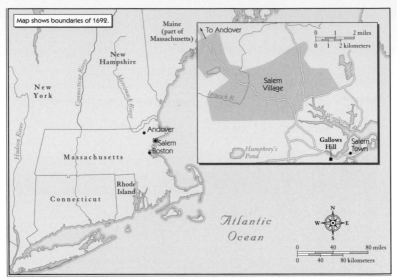

This map shows Massachusetts Bay colony and Salem in 1692.

## Samuel Parris

Salem Village, Massachusetts
February 26, 1692

Parris knew that some people in Salem Village believed witchcraft was at work in the town. He had seen how much worse Abigail and Betty were, and heard their claims that Tituba was the cause. So he called in several other ministers. One of them was John Hale from the nearby town of Beverly.

"I haven't seen anything like it," Hale told Parris. "The way their arms and necks twist and turn.

There's something not natural about it."

"That's what I thought," Parris replied. "It's like what happened to those Goodwin children a few years ago." Many people in Massachusetts knew about the Goodwins, who had been tormented by a woman who confessed to being a witch. She was hanged for her crime.

Hale, Parris, and the other men then called in Tituba and asked her what she knew about witchcraft. She explained that she had baked a witch cake to see if a witch was harming the girls. "But I am no witch," she said.

Soon Parris heard disturbing news. Two other girls in the village had also become sick and claimed they had been attacked by witches.

## Ann Putnam

Salem Village, Massachusetts
February 27, 1692

Ann Putnam lived about a mile away from the Parrises. The 12-year-old knew Abigail and Betty. She also knew that some people in the village disliked Mr. Parris. Her father, though, was one of the important men in the village who supported the minister. For two days, she had been feeling pains in her body and sensed a specter around her. This day, the specter told Ann her name: "I am Sarah Good."

Ann and others in the village knew Sarah Good. She often begged for money to feed her children, and she was known to have a bad temper. Good was also known to curse at people who refused to give her money. Even some of her own relatives didn't want to help her.

Two days later, the Putnam family and some of their friends met in the Putnam home to pray for Ann.

"It must be witchcraft," Mr. Putnam said. "Just as with Abigail and Betty." As the adults prayed, Ann said she could see Sarah Good, Tituba, and a third woman, Sarah Osborne, as plain as day. No one else in the house could see the three women. But they could see the terror on Ann's face. "No!" she cried. "Get back!"

"What's wrong, Ann?" her father asked.

"They have a knife!" Ann screamed. "They want to kill me!"

Mr. Putnam made a decision. "Something must be done," he said. "We must go to the magistrates and file a legal complaint. There are witches here in Salem, and we must get rid of them."

## Sarah Good

Salem Village, Massachusetts
March 1, 1692

The constable had come for the beggar, Sarah Good, that morning. Now she watched the meetinghouse fill up. It seemed the people of Salem were curious to see the three accused witches— Sarah Good, Sarah Osborne, and Tituba. Among those gathered were four girls who claimed to be afflicted: Abigail Williams, Betty Parris, Ann Putnam, and Elizabeth Hubbard.

Good knew the people of Salem disliked her. But was it her fault she had gone into debt years ago and now had to beg to survive? She had a 4-year-old daughter to feed and was pregnant with another child. Her husband, William, had sold their land

to try to pay what they owed. Now he struggled
to find work. Yes, she sometimes cursed those
who wouldn't help her. But if they were such good

The accusations of the children against people in the community led to the Salem witch trials.

Christians, she thought, how could they turn their backs on someone in need?

The legal hearing this day was not a trial.

Instead, Salem officials were trying to gather information to see if Good and the others should be brought to trial. During this questioning, Good faced the magistrates alone. Neither she nor any of the others accused had lawyers to help defend them. So, after prayers, magistrate John Hathorne began to question her.

"Why do you hurt these children?" Hathorne asked.

"I do not hurt them," Good said.

"Then you have someone in your power that you use to hurt them," Hathorne responded.

"I do not!" Good said. "I am falsely accused."

Hathorne turned to the four afflicted girls. "Is she one of the people who is tormenting you?" he asked.

"Yes, yes," the girls cried out. Good watched in disbelief as they began to thrash in their seats, as if some invisible being was torturing them.

"Why do you torment them?" Hathorne demanded.

"I do not torment them!" Good replied. "It was Sarah Osborne."

"Ask her husband," someone called out. "He's said himself she might be a witch."

Hathorne now turned to William Good. "Is this true?"

"I, I do not say my wife is a witch," William replied. Then Good listened in disbelief as he said, "But sometimes she does not treat me well, and I think that she is an enemy to all that is good."

## Tituba

Salem Village, Massachusetts
March 1, 1692

As the constable led Tituba into the meetinghouse, the enslaved woman glanced at Betty, Abigail, and the other girls. When she did, the girls began to moan and twitch in their seats.

"What evil spirits do you work with?" Hathorne asked her.

"None," Tituba replied.

"Have you ever seen the devil?" Hathorne continued.

Tituba's testimony against women in Salem Town was key to the trials.

"The devil came to me once and asked me to help him," she said. "And I saw four women who were working for him, hurting the children. I don't know them all, but two of them were Sarah Good and Sarah Osborne."

Tituba then said that she had hurt the children because the witches threatened to hurt her if she did not. She described how the witches sometimes took the form of animals and told her to harm the children.

She spoke of Sarah Osborne sending a creature with a woman's head, two legs, and wings. Tituba added, "Abigail Williams said she saw the same creature and then it turned into Osborne."

As Tituba talked, Abigail and the other girls once again began to cry out in pain. "Who is hurting the girls now?" Hathorne asked. "It is Sarah Good," Tituba replied. Later, she said she had met the devil and he showed her his book. Witches signed this book. Once they did, it was like a contract that made them servants of the devil. Sarah Good and Sarah Osborne had signed the book, Tituba said. She said she had too. In all, she saw nine marks in the book, meaning at least nine witches could be near.

The Puritans thought that Satan came to town in the form of witches.

# MORE ARE
# ACCUSED

# Ann Putnam

With the three accused witches under arrest, Ann's pains seemed to fade a bit. But soon she saw another specter coming to torment her. She felt something around her neck, trying to choke her. "She is trying to kill me!" Ann cried.

"Who is doing this?" Mr. Putnam asked.

"It is Dorothy Good, Sarah Good's daughter," Ann said. "Now she is biting and pinching me! Stop, stop!"

"But she is just a child of four," Mr. Putnam said.

"It is her, I know it," Ann said, thrashing her arms through the air.

The Putnams watched helplessly as their daughter cried out, "No, no, I won't do it!"

"Do what?" Mrs. Putnam asked.

"She wants me to sign the devil's book, but I won't do it!" Ann cried.

"Yes, resist, my child, resist," her father said.

For more than a week, Ann continued to see new specters coming to harm her. One was Elizabeth Proctor, the wife of John Proctor. He was a wealthy farmer in town. Another was Martha Corey. Mr. Putnam seemed shocked when Ann accused her of being a witch.

"But she is a faithful member of the church," he said. "And she must be close to 70 years old."

"I know it is her," Ann told her father. "She is after me!"

## Martha Corey

Salem Village, Massachusetts
March 12, 1692

Martha Corey was alone in her home. Her husband, Giles, had gone out for the day. When

Martha Corey was among the many women accused of withcraft.

the first women were accused of witchcraft,
Martha had scoffed at the idea. She still doubted
that witches were at work in Salem, but she
knew others believed it.

Corey heard a knock at the door. She opened it to see Edward Putnam, an uncle of Ann's. Next to him was his neighbor, Ezekiel Cheever.

"I know why you've come," she said. "Someone in the village thinks I'm a witch."

"Not just anyone," Putnam said. "It's my niece, Ann. She said she has seen your specter all around her."

"You know that I have stated my belief in Jesus Christ," Corey said. "I am a faithful member of the church."

Cheever now spoke up. "Yes, that is what you say, but we can't see into your heart. We all know that witches have sometimes crept into congregations, saying they are children of God."

"God has left us during these troubled times," Corey said. "And the devil is among us. But he's not in me. I am not a witch."

# Mary Warren

Salem Village, Massachusetts
March 12, 1692

Mary Warren, the 20-year-old who worked as a maid for John and Elizabeth Proctor, thought she saw a form coming toward her. The specter sat in her lap, and it looked like Mr. Proctor.

"What is it?" she cried out.

Proctor was actually across the room. "There's nothing there," he said. "It's just my shadow."

"Who said that?" Warren asked. "I can't see anything but this specter on my lap."

"Come on, Mary," Proctor said. "Get busy with your chores. That will make you forget this foolishness of specters. And if that doesn't work," he continued angrily, "then maybe I'll just have to beat you if you see more specters."

Warren tried to snap out of her trance. But when Proctor was away, she felt afflicted again.

# Ann Putnam

Salem Village, Massachusetts
March 15, 1692

After the Sunday church service, the Putnam family gathered around the dining room table. Ann stared at a chair. "There is someone here," she said. "I see a specter at the table."

"Who is it?" her mother asked.

"I don't know," Ann said. "But I have seen her at the meetinghouse. I don't think she lives in the village. She comes over from Salem Town. And she is old."

Mrs. Putnam and the family servant, Mercy Lewis, suggested some names. Ann shook her head at each of them. Finally, Lewis said, "Could it be Rebecca Nurse?"

"Yes!" Ann said. "Rebecca Nurse."

"But she is a good Christian, one of the best in Salem," Mr. Putnam said.

"You said the same of Martha Corey," Ann

said. "I say I see Rebecca Nurse now, and Corey has tormented me before."

The next day, Ann watched as her father led Martha Corey into the main room of the Putnam home. Immediately, Ann fell to the floor in a fit, her body parts twisting wildly. "She is the cause of this," Ann cried, pointing at Corey. Then Ann said she saw a yellow bird sucking at Corey's hand. Corey rubbed her hand, and Ann said, "Oh, it is gone now."

Ann next called out, "I see a man being roasted over open flames in the fireplace. And it is you, Martha Corey, turning the spit that holds him." Mercy Lewis took a stick and swung twice at the fireplace, where Ann said the man was burning. "Watch out," Ann called to Lewis. "Corey's specter is after you!" In an instant, Lewis was on the floor, as if tormented by the specter. As the girls shrieked in pain, Putnam led Corey out of the house.

Over the next few days, Ann continued to suffer. She was certain that Corey and Nurse were to blame.

# Deodat Lawson

Salem Village, Massachusetts
March 20, 1692

Standing in the Salem Village meetinghouse, Deodat Lawson saw many familiar faces. Just before Samuel Parris had been hired, Lawson had been the minister there. Lawson had heard the strange tales of the afflicted girls and the belief that witchcraft was the cause. He returned to the village to see for himself what was happening.

The night before, while visiting the Parrises at the parsonage, he saw Abigail Williams run through the house. She stretched out her arms as she ran, as if she were trying to fly. Then Abigail claimed that Rebecca Nurse was in the room, demanding that she sign the devil's book. Abigail refused, but she ran through the house crazily, taking burning sticks from the fire and throwing them around.

Reverend Parris had asked Lawson to lead the service this Sunday. Looking out over the congregation, Lawson saw Abigail and several other afflicted girls. Martha Corey was also there. As Lawson spoke, Abigail interrupted him. "Look at the beam above the reverend! There is Martha Corey with her little yellow bird!" Lawson looked where the girl was pointing but saw nothing. Then Ann Putnam cried out, "I see another bird sitting on the reverend's hat!" People sitting near the girls quieted them, so Lawson could go on with his service.

The next day, Lawson returned to the meetinghouse to watch the first legal questioning of Martha Corey. The room was packed with residents eager to hear her answer whether she was a witch.

"Why do you afflict these children?" Joseph Hathorne asked.

"I do not afflict them," Corey replied. Lawson watched as some of the afflicted spoke out against Corey, claiming that her specter had tormented them. There must have been about 10 afflicted people by then, Lawson guessed. Some women had also stepped forward, joining the younger girls who had first claimed to be tormented. When the questioning was over, Corey was taken to the local jail. Lawson noticed that when Corey left the meetinghouse, the afflicted calmed down.

## Rebecca Nurse

Salem Village, Massachusetts
March 24, 1692

Rebecca Nurse entered the meetinghouse knowing the people who accused her of witchcraft would be waiting for her. As soon as she entered the building, some of them began to have fits. The accusers included Ann Putnam and Abigail Williams. When asked if she had harmed them or others, Nurse said, "I never afflicted no child, never in my life."

But children weren't the only accusers. Mrs. Putnam, Ann's mother, said Nurse had also tormented her. She cried out in the meetinghouse, "Didn't you bring Satan with you? Didn't you tempt me to deny God?"

Rebecca Nurse maintained her innocence when questioned about
being a witch.

"I am innocent!" Nurse exclaimed, but more girls yelled out in pain. Others in the meetinghouse began to cry, flailing and wailing in agony. "Look," one girl shouted, "I can see the devil whispering in her ear right now!"

Nurse continued to proclaim her innocence, but the afflicted girls just shouted and cried even louder. The magistrates had seen and heard enough. Soon, Nurse was led to jail.

## Deodat Lawson

Salem Village, Massachusetts
March 24, 1692

The minister had heard some of the questioning of Rebecca Nurse but had left the meetinghouse before it ended. In the street, he was shocked to hear the shrieks and screeching the afflicted made. Later in the afternoon, Lawson returned to give the weekly lecture. Ministers across the area took turns giving this religious talk. With the fear of witches and the devil gripping Salem, he talked about Satan's power to harm anyone. Yet he also reminded the people that no one had been proven guilty of being a witch. He told them that no one should falsely accuse anyone else of being a witch.

**3**

# STILL MORE ARE QUESTIONED

The women accused of witchcraft were all questioned by men.

# Samuel Parris

In the weeks since Tituba and John Indian had baked the witch cake, Samuel Parris learned a disturbing fact. His neighbor Mary Sibley had directed them to bake it. Parris told Sibley to come to the parsonage to discuss the matter.

"You don't deny that it was your idea to bake the witch cake?" Parris asked.

"No sir," Sibley replied.

"And you know that it is a form of magic, which can open the door to the evils of Satan?" Parris continued.

"I see that now, Mr. Parris. I see how the spread of witchcraft has come after that day," Sibley said.

"But I didn't know that before. It was just something I knew people did to try to find a witch."

Mr. Parris picked up a piece of paper. "I have written a statement to read before the whole congregation. It says that you will accept the blame for your part in the evil that now surrounds us. Will you confess your sin and ask for forgiveness?" The minister saw tears fill Sibley's eyes and stream down her cheeks.

"Yes, Mr. Parris, I will," she said.

Two days later was Sunday. Speaking to a full meetinghouse, Parris read the confession he had written for Sibley. He also told the congregation that even members of a church could be under the devil's spell. After all, the accusations against Martha Corey and Rebecca Nurse showed this.

# Mary Warren

Salem Village, Massachusetts
April 19, 1692

The torments that Mary Warren suffered had ended. She posted a note on the meetinghouse door telling the congregation this happy news. She asked the people to offer prayers of thanks to God. The next day, Sunday, Samuel Parris read the note to the congregation. After the service, Parris asked Warren what had been going on with the other girls.

"I think they are lying," she replied. "Or what they thought was real was just something in their heads. I can see that now—it was all an illusion."

But while Warren declared herself free from torment, her employers, Elizabeth and John Proctor, were soon among the accused. Many people in the village came forward to say Mr. and Mrs. Proctor tormented them.

And on April 18 Warren found herself accused of witchcraft. The next day, Warren joined several others who were accused of afflicting Ann Putnam, Abigail Williams, and several other girls. The accused witches included Martha Corey's husband, Giles, and Abigail Hobbs, a teenager from the neighboring village of Topsfield. When Warren was questioned, the afflicted girls immediately began having fits.

When asked if she were guilty of witchcraft, Warren replied, "I am innocent."

After a few more questions, Warren fell to the floor, suffering a fit of her own. "I am sorry for what I have done," she said, in between the spasms she suffered. She called out to God to help her, but as she tried to say more, her mouth shut and her body kept twitching. Finally, she managed to say, "I will tell, I will tell, those other witches made me practice witchcraft too."

"Have you signed the devil's book?" Joseph Hathorne asked. Warren blurted out, "No." And all the time Warren suffered her fits, the afflicted girls behaved normally—their own fits had stopped.

# Bridget Bishop

Salem, Massachusetts
April 19, 1692

After Mary Warren, Bridget Bishop was questioned next. Like Sarah Good, Bishop had often faced difficult times. When she was married years before, she and her husband sometimes fought. One time they called each other names in public. For punishment they were forced to stand in the Salem Town marketplace with gags in their mouths. Bishop had also been accused

Children had fits that they said were caused by witches.

of witchcraft years before, but nothing came of it. Now, she stood in the meetinghouse and heard Ann Putnam and the others accuse her of tormenting them.

When questioned, she said she had never seen the girls before. She explained that she had never been to Salem Village and had never spoken with a devil. But with every shake of her head, the girls cried out in agony. Another accuser said that Bishop's specter had come to the village. The accuser said her brother had swung his sword at the specter's skirt. She said they could hear the blade rip through the fabric. Magistrate Hathorne asked that Bishop's skirt be checked. They found a small tear in the fabric.

When the questioning ended, a bystander asked her, "Doesn't it trouble you to see the girls suffer so much?"

"No, it doesn't," Bishop replied.

"But don't you think some witch is tormenting them?" the man asked.

"I don't know what to think," Bishop said.

# Mary Warren

Salem Town, Massachusetts
April 21, 1692

Now that she had confessed to witchcraft, Warren sat in the Salem Town jail, where the magistrates questioned her again. She described how her employer, John Proctor, had brought a book to her. She thought it was a Bible, but as soon as she touched a page, her finger left a black mark. She described how he threatened to burn her with hot tongs from the fireplace. During the questioning, Warren sometimes went into fits, claiming she saw the specters of the Proctors.

"How do you know Mrs. Proctor is a witch?" one of the magistrates asked.

"She told me she signed the devil's book," Warren replied.

"Have you seen any other witches since you have been in jail?" the magistrate continued.

"Yes," Warren said. "The specters of Martha Corey and Sarah Good have come to me."

The magistrates asked Warren if the Proctors had stuck pins into poppets. These were little dolls, not puppets, that witches used to try to hurt real people. She said no, but she had heard them talk about that form of witchcraft.

## George Burroughs

Salem Town, Massachusetts
May 5, 1692

The Reverend George Burroughs sat in a room at a local tavern. The minister had once served the congregation in Salem Village. Like other ministers there, he had argued with some church members over his pay. Thomas Putnam, father of the afflicted Ann, was one of his main foes.

Burroughs now served as the minister in Wells, Maine. He had been arrested there two days before. He had been accused of witchcraft by the afflicted Salem Village girls. One of them was Mercy Lewis, the Putnams' servant, who had worked for Burroughs as a servant in Maine before she came to Salem. Maine was part of

Massachusetts Bay Colony at the time. Like many residents of Maine, Lewis had seen the horrors of the fighting there. Both of her parents had been killed by the Wabanaki Indians.

On May 9 Burroughs appeared before the judges. Local magistrates Joseph Hathorne and Jonathan Corwin were joined by two judges from Boston, William Stoughton and Samuel Sewall. At first the judges met with Burroughs in private. One said, "We hear that you never take communion, even though you are a member of the church in Roxbury."

"It has been a long time since I had communion, I know," Burroughs replied.

"That is odd, isn't it?" the judge asked. "You are a minister, yet you never take communion. And you have not even baptized some of your children."

"That is true." Burroughs could tell that the men did not think he was a good Puritan.

The public questioning soon began. Burroughs saw afflicted girls go into fits as he entered the courtroom. The court then read statements the afflicted had already given about Burroughs. One girl said that the ghosts of Burroughs's first two wives had appeared to her. The ghosts said that the minister had killed them. Other girls spoke out about how his specter had tormented them. The girls were sure Burroughs was a wizard—a male witch. They described how he asked them to sign the devil's book. Another witness, Elizer Keyser, said she thought Burroughs was the ringleader of all the witches.

To Burroughs, everything he heard was shocking. He told the judges, "I don't understand any of this."

## William Phips

Boston, Massachusetts
May 27, 1692

It had been just two weeks since Sir William Phips had returned to Boston from London. He arrived carrying a charter, a document from King William and Queen Mary of England.

The charter spelled out the kind of government that would rule the colony of Massachusetts Bay. The colony could still pass its own laws as long as they did not violate any laws in England. Along with granting the charter, William and Mary had named Phips the governor of Massachusetts Bay.

Phips had been born in Maine, and he had spent time as a ship's captain. In 1687 he had discovered a sunken Spanish ship loaded with treasure. His share of the find made him a rich man and an important figure in the colony.

Upon returning from London and becoming governor, Phips learned about the witch scare gripping the Salem area. Dozens of people were being held in jail in Boston and elsewhere, accused of being witches. Phips met with his council, which advised him on how to run the colony.

William Stoughton was the deputy governor, second only to Phips. "We must do something," he told Phips. "We're running out of room in the jails, and some of the people have been there for months."

Huge crowds gathered to hear testimony against the men and women accused of witchcraft.

"I will set up a special court," Phips said, "and Stoughton, I'm putting you in charge of it." Phips named other men to act as judges for the court, including Salem magistrates John Hathorne and Jonathan Corwin. Phips and the council decided that the court would hear cases dealing with "all manner of crime and offenses."

Later, Phips wrote to royal officials in London about his first acts as governor. But he did not mention the court or the accused witches in Salem. The new governor did not want English officials to think there were any serious problems in Massachusetts Bay.

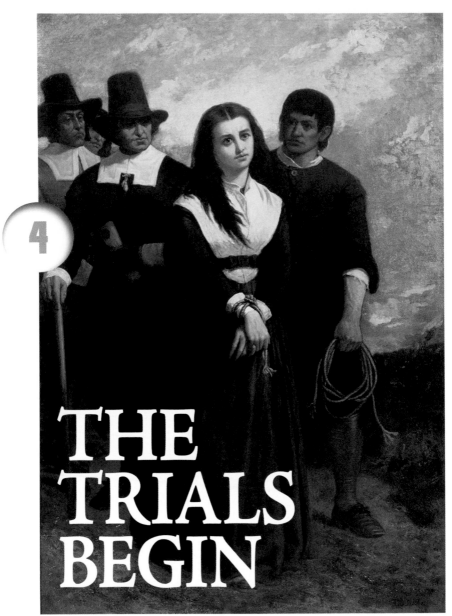

**4**

# THE TRIALS BEGIN

Bridget Bishop was the first woman accused of witchcraft to be convicted at trial.

# Bridget Bishop

Salem Town, Massachusetts
June 2, 1692

Bridget Bishop was the first accused witch to go on trial. Before Bishop left her jail cell, a group of women came and told her to undress.

"Why should I do that?" she asked.

"We need to search your body for witch marks—any unusual marks that mean you are working for the devil," one woman said.

Bishop did as they ordered. She was shocked when the women claimed to see unusual bits of skin hanging from her body.

Next, Bishop was led to the meetinghouse. There the afflicted girls described how her specter had tormented them and tried to make them sign the devil's book. Their fits continued throughout the trial. Then people from Salem told how over the years she had appeared before them when they awoke. They said she tried to harm them. One of the accusers was John Cook.

"It was six years ago," he said. "I was still in bed, and I saw her in my room, grinning at me. Then she smacked me in the head. She appeared to me later that day, but no one else could see her, only me."

John Bly and his son William accused Bishop in a statement. They said William had found poppets when he went to do work on the Bishop home. The dolls were filled with headless pins.

Bishop asserted her innocence to the court, but the jury of residents found her guilty of witchcraft.

## Bridget Bishop

Salem Town, Massachusetts
June 10, 1692

For a week Bridget Bishop sat in the Salem jail, waiting for her execution day. The time in jail had been hard for her and the other prisoners. The building was cold, dark, and damp. It had an overpowering smell of human waste and unwashed bodies. The conditions only got worse as more accused witches filled the jail. Now Bishop would have a chance to breathe fresh air—for the last time.

Sheriff George Corwin and some of his men came for Bishop before noon. "Aren't you the lucky one," one of the jailers said. "You get to be the first witch hanged."

Bishop was silent as the men put her in a cart. Some rode on horseback and others walked as they led her to a field on the edge of Salem Town. Bishop saw people come out of their homes to follow her to the gallows. Some of the afflicted girls came out too, and they twitched and screamed as Bishop passed. Finally, the cart reached the spot where a rope had been prepared for the execution.

Some of the sheriff's men tied her hands behind her back and tied her legs together.

With the noose now around her neck, Bishop called out, "I am innocent! I am not a witch!" She stood on a ladder. In an instant, one of the men pushed it away, leaving Bishop to dangle from the rope until she was dead.

## Cotton Mather

Boston, Massachusetts
June 15, 1692

From Boston, Cotton Mather had been closely following the events in Salem. The son of the minister Increase Mather and a minister himself, Mather had some experience with the evils of witchcraft. In 1688 he had gone to examine the Goodwin children of Boston. They claimed a woman named Goody Glover had afflicted them. Mather wrote about the case the following year—after Glover was hanged as a witch. Mather had a keen interest in what he called the Invisible World—a world where specters and devils could harm innocent Puritans.

Cotton Mather

Massachusetts governor Phips asked Mather
and several other Boston ministers about the
events in Salem. Phips was concerned that the
accused might not be getting fair trials. Writing
for all the ministers, Mather prepared a document.

MEMORABLE PROVIDENCES,

Relating to

# WITCHCRAFTS
## And POSSESSIONS.

A Faithful Account of many Wonderful and Surprising Things, that have befallen several *Bewitched* and *Possessed* Persons in *New-England*.

Particularly, A NARRATIVE of the marvellous *Trouble* and *Releef* Experienced by a pious Family in *Boston*, very lately, and sadly molested with EVIL SPIRITS.

*Whereunto is added,*

A Discourse delivered unto a Congregation in *Boston*, on the Occasion of that *Illustrious Providence*. As also

A Discourse delivered unto the same Congregation, on the occasion of an horrible *Self-Murder* Committed in the Town.

With an *Appendix*, in vindication of a Chapter in a late Book of Remarkable Providences, from the Calumnies of a Quaker at *Pen-silvania*.

*Written* By Cotton Mather, *Minister of the Gospel.*

And Recommended by the Ministers of *Boston* and *Charleston*

Printed at *Boston* in *N. England* by *R. P.* 1689.
Sold by *Joseph Brunning*, at his Shop at the Corner of the *Prison-Lane* next the *Exchange*.

In this document, Cotton Mather detailed how those accused of witchcraft should be treated.

In it he outlined how the religious leaders thought the Salem court should handle the trial. Mather wrote that the court should show "an exceeding tenderness" toward the accused, especially if they had not previously done wrong. He warned against taking spectral evidence—claims that the afflicted might make about being harmed by a specter. Satan, Mather believed, could use the image of an innocent person to torment people. To him this meant that spectral evidence was not proof that someone was a witch.

Instead, Mather thought the judges should consider older, standard legal writings that explained how to determine if someone was a witch. One method was to search for witch marks on an accused person. Another was a witness hearing an accused person—not the specter of the accused—cast a spell. If someone confessed to being a witch, that was also proof. Still, Mather believed witches were a real threat. He wanted the trials to go ahead as quickly as possible.

George Burroughs recited the Lord's Prayer before his execution in an attempt to prove his innocence.

# THE TRIALS CONTINUE

# 5

# Sarah Good

Boston, Massachusetts
June 28, 1692

Since her arrest months before, Sarah Good had sat in the jail in Boston. The harsh conditions there were made worse knowing that her 4-year-old daughter Dorothy had also been arrested as an accused witch. Good had given birth to another daughter, Mercy, while in the jail. The infant had died there. Now, Good had been brought back to Salem to stand trial.

She listened as she was accused of afflicting three people, including Ann Putnam. Then depositions from others were read. Some people said her specter had tormented them while Good was in the Boston jail.

Rebecca Nurse had many defenders who believed that she was innocent.

Others said that Good herself had cursed them or otherwise treated them badly several years before. Mary Walcott was a teenager who had named several people as witches. She stated in her deposition that she had often seen Good's specter with other witches. "She tried to force me to sign the devil's book," Walcott added.

When the trial was over, Sarah Good heard the jury foreman declare her guilty. She would soon follow Bridget Bishop to the gallows.

## Rebecca Nurse

Salem Town, Massachusetts
June 29, 1692

Although she was accused of witchcraft, Rebecca Nurse was glad to know that some Salem residents believed in her innocence. As her trial began, she listened as those people defended her. Others attacked the character of her accusers. Joseph Fowler said that Sarah Bibber, one of those who had named Nurse as a witch, was a troublemaker. "She's always spreading gossip and trying to make mischief between people," he said.

Chief Justice William Stoughton presided over Rebecca Nurse's trial.

Sarah Nurse, Rebecca's daughter-in-law, had stronger proof against Bibber. During the trial, Bibber had once grabbed her knee in pain and blamed it on Rebecca Nurse. But Sarah Nurse testified, "I saw what she did. Sarah Bibber had a pin hidden in her clothing. She took it out and stabbed herself, and then blamed my mother-in-law!"

Many more people stepped forward to defend Nurse. She felt a wave of relief when the jury found her not guilty. But as soon as the verdict was said, the afflicted in the courtroom began to scream. The judges at this point took a break. Nurse had no choice but to wait until they returned. She then heard Chief Justice William Stoughton say, "I would like the jurors to consider again what happened when Deliverance and Abigail Hobbs testified today."

When the Hobbs women had appeared to speak against Nurse, she had cried out, "What, they are going to speak against me, when they are like me?" Nurse meant that they were accused of witchcraft, like her, not that they were witches.

Thomas Fisk, foreman of the jury, spoke up. He looked first at the judges, and then at her. Nurse could tell he was speaking to her, but her hearing was not good, and she was not feeling well. She couldn't understand what Fisk was saying. Afraid she might say the wrong thing, she didn't reply to Fisk's question. The jury then went out to consider their verdict again. When they returned, Fisk spoke up. "We find the defendant guilty of witchcraft."

Nurse's supporters moaned in disbelief. "Didn't you understand what was happening, what they asked you?" someone asked her. Nurse shook her head no. The friend explained, "He asked what you meant when you said the Hobbses were like you. Did you mean you and they are witches, or all just merely accused?"

"Just that we are accused," Nurse said. "You know that I'm not a witch!"

Nurse realized that she had lost the chance to say what she meant. Now she would hang for being a witch.

The witchcraft trials were noisy, with people crying out and making accusations.

# William Phips

Boston, Massachusetts
July 1692

William Phips looked at the documents in front of him. All concerned the conviction of Rebecca Nurse. Almost 40 people had signed a statement protesting the Salem court's rejection of the jury's initial not-guilty ruling.

Nurse also wrote out a statement explaining a comment she had made when she saw the Hobbses in court. She said that she intended her comment to mean that they were all accused, not that they were really witches. The governor decided to spare her life. Nurse would not hang.

But soon Phips received more news from Salem. It seemed that when his decision to spare Nurse reached the town, the afflicted had erupted into fits once again. Important citizens in the town were convinced that Nurse was a witch. Phips changed his mind. Nurse would hang after all.

## Sarah Good

Salem Town, Massachusetts
July 19, 1692

Sheriff George Corwin and his men came to the Salem jail. "It's time to go," the sheriff called to Good and the other women who were going to be hanged that day. Good joined the others in the cart that would take them to the gallows. Along the way, the women prayed.

People convicted of witchcraft were sometimes hanged two at a time.

As the sheriff's men put the rope around Good's neck, Reverend Nicholas Noyes of Salem Town came to her. "The court has found you guilty," Noyes said. "You should confess your sin."

"I have not committed any sin," Good replied. "At least nothing that should lead to my death."

"I know you are a witch, Sarah Good," he continued. "Confess, so you won't also be a liar."

"You are a liar. I am no more a witch than you are a wizard. If you take away my life, God will give you blood to drink." Good knew that Noyes would know she was referring to a part of the Bible describing ways God will punish sinners. With those last words, the rope tightened around Good's neck, and soon she would be dead.

## Mary Warren

Salem, Massachusetts
July 20, 1692

After she confessed to being a witch, the magistrates of Salem released Mary Warren from jail. Confessing to witchcraft was one way to avoid immediate hanging. Under English law, Warren knew she could still be hanged. But for now the officials in Salem were ready to let her and other confessed witches live. The officials thought the released witches could provide evidence against other accused witches. Warren did not disappoint them. After she was released, she began to accuse more people of being witches.

This day in court, several accused witches from Andover, Massachusetts, faced questioning. Warren watched as 18-year-old Ann Lacy was brought into the meetinghouse. Immediately, Warren began to twitch and shout. Lacy touched Warren's arm and the fit stopped. This had happened to Warren before—when an accused witch touched her, her fits stopped. This "touch test" was now common in the trials. It told the judges that the accused was probably a witch if she could end Warren's suffering simply by touching her.

A magistrate said, "You are accused of practicing witchcraft. Can you look at Mary Warren in a friendly way and not torment her?"

Warren saw Lacy glance at her, and her fits started again. Warren soon collapsed to the floor.

"Do you admit now that you are a witch?" Still on the floor, Warren heard Lacy say yes. She described how she had afflicted Warren and several others. As Lacy went on, Warren cried out, "I see a man, a little man, on the table!"

Lacy said it was the specter of a wizard she knew. She described seeing this man and many other witches sharing a meal with Satan.

As Lacy's confession went on, Warren's fits calmed. She took Lacy's hand, and both young women cried as Lacy said, "Oh, Mary, can you forgive me for what I have done?"

"Yes, I forgive you," said Warren.

## John Proctor

Salem Town, Massachusetts
July 23, 1692

As he sat in jail, John Proctor began to write a letter. Since his arrest weeks before, he had heard about the trials and executions of the first people found guilty of witchcraft. His own trial would be coming soon. Proctor addressed his letter to some of the ministers of Boston, including Increase Mather, the father of Cotton Mather. Proctor wrote that he and the others with him in jail were innocent. But, he continued, the Salem officials were already convinced of their guilt.

They and the people in general, he wrote, were "so much enraged and incensed against us by the works of the Devil." Proctor claimed that several accused wizards, including his own son, had been tortured so they would confess to crimes.

Proctor asked the ministers to use their influence with the government. He wanted future trials moved to Boston, if possible. If not, then at least the ministers could try to arrange to have new judges sent to Salem. He asked them to attend one of the trials and observe the goings-on. He wrote, "You may be the means of saving the shedding [of] our innocent bloods."

## Increase Mather

Boston, Massachusetts
August 1, 1692

In the Harvard College library, Increase Mather met with other ministers. He held up the letter they had received from John Proctor.

"What should we do about this?" Mather asked the ministers.

Many ministers were unhappy with some of the evidence offered at the trials, but none followed Cotton Mather's suggestions to fix the problem.

"What can we do?" one of the ministers replied.

Mather and the others were already uncomfortable with some of the evidence used in Salem. In particular, they disliked how the judges relied on spectral evidence. The letter Cotton Mather had written earlier, speaking out against that kind of evidence, had been ignored. The ministers decided that Increase Mather should now write a more detailed report on this form of evidence. But the men did nothing to move the trials, as Proctor had requested, or to look for new judges.

## Deodat Lawson

Salem Town, Massachusetts
August 5, 1692

With Increase Mather next to him, Deodat Lawson waited for the trial of Reverend George Burroughs to begin. Lawson had a particular interest in hearing the case against Burroughs. When questioned earlier, Ann Putnam had said that the ghosts of Lawson's wife and child had appeared to her. They had been killed several years before. She said the ghosts blamed their deaths on Burroughs. During the earlier questioning, Putnam and another girl also reported seeing the ghosts of Burroughs's first two wives. They also accused the minister of using witchcraft to help the Wabanaki Indians of Maine battle the Puritans there.

This day, Lawson heard the witnesses describe how Burroughs had tormented them and tried to make them sign the devil's book. One of the afflicted said that Burroughs had told her he was not just a wizard, but a conjurer. The accuser said he had claimed to have even greater powers. Lawson also heard the afflicted describe how Burroughs wanted the witches he recruited to secretly torment the people of Salem. He led meetings where the witches gathered and received his orders.

At one point the judges separated the witnesses so they could not hear what the others were saying. But several agreed that the ghost of Lawson's wife and child were in the courtroom. They accused Burroughs of killing them.

"But I do not see any ghosts," Burroughs said.

The evidence against Burroughs mounted, and by day's end, the jury found him guilty.

"What do you think of all this?" Lawson asked Increase Mather.

"If I were a juror, I would have voted for his guilt too," Mather replied. "What about you?"

Lawson said, "I think anyone who heard all that

happened today would know the power that Satan uses to try to deceive good Christians."

## Cotton Mather

Salem Town, Massachusetts
August 19, 1692

Although he had not attended any of the trials, Cotton Mather traveled to Salem. He had come to watch the hangings of convicted witches. Mather sat on horseback at the place some were now calling Gallows Hill, the site of the previous hangings. He was particularly curious to see how a fellow minister would act as his death approached. Joining George Burroughs on the gallows that day were John Proctor and three other witches. Mather had learned that Proctor's wife, Elizabeth, had escaped her execution for now. She was pregnant, so she remained in a cell in Boston. She would hang after her baby was born.

Mather was part of a large crowd that came out that day to watch the hangings. One by one, the five climbed the ladder to the gallows.

John Proctor, like the others, declared he was innocent. He looked over at Mather and said, "Please, Reverend Mather, say a prayer for me." Proctor continued, "I forgive the sins of those who have falsely accused me, and if there are real witches here in Salem, I hope God may help you all find them." The others said similar things just before they took their last breaths.

When Burroughs stood on the ladder, he began to pray. He finished with the Lord's Prayer: "Our father, who art in heaven . . ."

Some people in the crowd began to cry. Mather realized that Burroughs was trying to prove his innocence by saying this prayer. Some people believed a true witch could not say the words to this prayer, first spoken by Jesus. But then some of the afflicted girls cried out, "Look, the devil is on his shoulder. The devil is telling him the words!"

Mather then spoke up. "The devil can take many forms," he said. "He can even appear to be an angel, if he chooses. And he can certainly take the form of a minister." This seemed to calm the crowd, or at least those who might have begun to think Burroughs could be innocent. Then, Burroughs, the so-called ringleader of the witches, was executed.

## Giles Corey

Salem Town, Massachusetts
September 9, 1692

After Giles Corey had spent several months in jail, the court heard the testimony of witnesses who described how he had afflicted them. His troubles had begun in the spring. At that time he had given testimony that suggested the charges against his wife, Martha, could be true. But the 80-year-old farmer later took back what he said. Soon after, he was accused of being a wizard. Now some of the afflicted said that his specter had tormented them even while he was jail. Ann Putnam said, "He almost choked me to death as he urged me to sign the Devil's book." Mary Warren described how he bit and pinched her.

Over the next week, Corey was formally accused
of witchcraft. He appeared before a grand jury,
which would decide if his case should go to trial.

Giles Corey was tried for witchcraft even though he refused to enter a plea.

He told the grand jury, "I am not guilty." He refused
to enter a plea.

One of the jurors asked, "Do you agree to stand

trial for this charge?" He did not answer.

Corey had decided to stand mute. Under English law, standing mute gave him the choice of not trying to prove his innocence in court. By custom, the jurors asked him three times if he would stand trial. Each time, he said no. Corey knew he could not get a fair trial. By standing mute, he was making a small protest against all the witch proceedings. But he knew that by refusing to stand trial, he faced a severe punishment.

As Corey sat in jail, a friend of his named Thomas Gardner came to visit him.

"You must stop this, Giles," Gardner said. "Go to court. Take the chance that the jury will find you innocent."

"I will not," Corey replied.

"Then you know what will happen," said Gardner.

"Let them press me to death," Giles said. "I am ready to die, but I will not die because of the lie that I am a wizard."

On September 19 Sheriff George Corwin

led Corey out of his cell and into a nearby field. Corwin and his men made Corey lie face up on a wooden board. They put another board on his chest, then began putting rocks on the board. Corey knew they expected him to change his mind, but he remained silent as the weight began to crush his chest.

"Will you stand trial?" Corwin asked.

With the stones pressing against him, Corey simply muttered, "More weight." At one point, his tongue drooped out of his mouth. Corwin pushed it back in with a stick. Soon everything went black for Corey.

## Cotton Mather

Boston, Massachusetts
September 20, 1692

In Boston, Cotton Mather continued to work on a project he had begun several weeks before. He wanted to write a thorough account of the Salem witch trials and witchcraft in general. He knew that more people were speaking out against the trials, and especially the use of spectral evidence.

He had asked the Salem judges about that form of evidence. They assured him that the court did not rely on that alone to convict the accused.

Now, Mather wrote a letter to Stephen Sewall, who was the clerk of the Salem court. The minister asked for trial records of many of the witches who had been found guilty. He also asked Sewall to write his own version of what he had seen and heard in court. Mather asked for Sewall's help so the minister could find a way to confront "the infernal enemy"—Satan. Mather would call his book *The Wonders of the Invisible World: Being an Account of the Trials of Several Witches Lately Executed in New England*.

Meanwhile, Increase Mather had finished his study of spectral evidence. On October 3 Cotton Mather joined other Boston-area ministers at Harvard College to hear a reading of Increase's study. Mather heard his father's arguments against spectral evidence. There was no question that Satan could take the form of an innocent person to try to persuade others to become witches. The elder Mather did not doubt that witches existed, in Massachusetts and elsewhere. But, he wrote, "It were better that ten suspected witches should escape, than that one innocent person should be condemned."

Governor William Phips

# 6

# THE END
# OF THE
# WITCH
# SCARE

# William Phips

Boston, Massachusetts
October 12, 1692

The governor knew that the words of the two Mathers about the Salem trials were being read across the colony. He knew more people were speaking out against the trials. Now, for the first time, he wrote to officials in England explaining what was happening in Salem and the surrounding towns.

He described the situation he had found when he returned to Massachusetts in May. He wrote about the afflicted and their families accusing others of witchcraft. He wrote, "The Devil had taken the name and shape of several persons who were doubtless innocent and to my certain knowledge of good reputation."

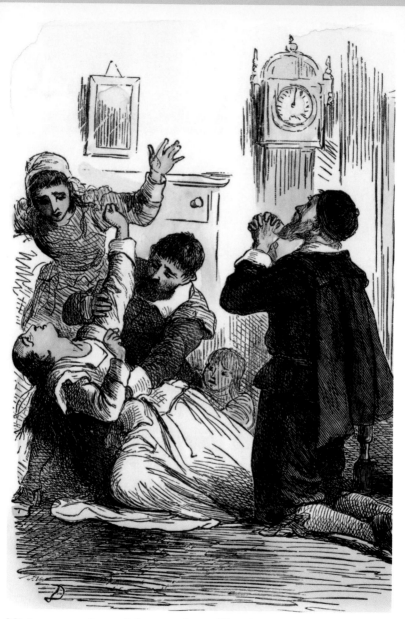

Ministers sometimes tried to save those afflicted by witchcraft with prayer.

Because of that, he was stopping the trials. He would wait to hear from the king and queen before starting them again. Phips did not mention that several weeks before, his wife, Mary, had been accused of witchcraft.

Soon after writing to the British officials, Phips received a letter from a group of men in Andover. Back in July afflicted girls from Salem Village had accused several Andover women of being witches. Many more had been accused since then. While the men writing Phips felt sure that witches were real, they believed several women in their town had been falsely accused. To make matters worse, the women felt pressured to confess to being witches, even though they were not. The men feared the false charges against women in the town would continue. The men did not ask the governor to do anything specific. Still, it was clear they hoped he could help solve the problem.

# Cotton Mather

Boston, Massachusetts
December 1692

The problem of witchcraft had spread to Boston. Several times, Cotton Mather went to visit Mercy Short, a girl in the city who seemed terribly afflicted. Short's parents and her three siblings had been killed by French and Indian forces in New Hampshire. For a time, those enemies had held her captive. Massachusetts Bay had paid a ransom to free her, and she ended up in Boston.

Mather had first heard of the girl's fits months before. They had started after Short went to the jail to give food and clothing to several of the accused witches. Now, for almost two weeks, she had barely eaten. On one of his visits, Mather had lost a ring that was in his pocket. Short told him, "The specters took it. But I know where they hid it." Mather went to the spot and found the ring.

"Be careful," Short told the minister, "because they will try to take it again."

On one visit Short asked Mather what she should say when Satan came to her. He referred to a passage in the Bible, saying, "Tell him that Jesus Christ has broken the serpent's head." The serpent meant Satan. But she was in the middle of a fit, and Short couldn't understand what he said.

By now, Mather's book, *The Wonders of the Invisible World,* had been published. Many people criticized his views. Some thought he didn't speak out strongly enough against the witches in Salem and elsewhere. Some wanted him to come out against the trials that sent innocent people to the gallows. Mather believed witches were real. And he could see the scars and burns on Short's body. But he warned others who heard Short say the names of her tormentors not to repeat them. He told them, "I don't want anyone to be falsely accused of being a witch."

# William Phips

Boston, Massachusetts
January 31, 1693

Although he had ended the Salem trials, Governor Phips was still not sure what to do next. The British government had not yet sent him instructions.

After Phips ended the trials, Massachusetts Bay had made some changes to its legal system. The colony's lawmakers met as a group in what was called the General Court. In December, the General Court had created new courts for the colony. The court that had heard the witch trials was designed to be temporary. The new court system would be permanent. The most powerful of the new courts was the Superior Court. The General Court instructed it to hear the cases of people still in jail for witchcraft or who had been recently accused.

The Superior Court began hearing cases in January. Before the end of the month, Phips received the verdicts from several trials. Eight people were scheduled to be executed. Five had been found guilty in the earlier trials, and three during the trial that had started in January. Phips thought over the advice of the government's top lawyer, Anthony Checkley.

"These three new ones all confessed to being witches," Checkley explained in a report. "But no one who had confessed before was sentenced to hang. I think these three are as innocent as the others."

Thinking about what Checkley said, Phips made a decision. He would free all eight of the accused witches. None of them would hang.

## Samuel Parris

Salem Village, Massachusetts
February 1693

For a time, Samuel Parris noticed that several people in the congregation had stopped going to church. All of them, he knew, had family members who had been hanged as witches.

Samuel Parris interrogated one of the last accused of witchcraft before the trials were ended.

# *Tituba*

Boston, Massachusetts
May 9, 1693

Since her confession more than a year ago, Tituba had sat in jail, first in Salem and then in Boston. On this day, she learned that she would not go on trial for witchcraft.

"The court said there is no evidence against you," her jailer explained.

"Even though I confessed?" she asked.

"A confession is no longer accepted as evidence," the man said. "The same thing for spectral evidence. The governor is releasing everyone still in jail who is charged with witchcraft. You're free to go—as soon as someone pays your bill."

Tituba knew Massachusetts Bay charged people held in jail, even if they were innocent. They had to pay a fee to be released.

"I hope my master, Mr. Parris, will pay for me," Tituba said. But in the weeks to come, she learned that Parris would not pay her fee. He decided to sell Tituba rather than continuing to enslave her, or having to pay for her release.

## Samuel Parris

Salem Village, Massachusetts
November 18, 1694

The minister's battle with members of his congregation who had suffered from the witch trials dragged on. His opponents had written to Governor Phips, asking him to help settle the dispute. After this, ministers in both Boston and Salem told Parris he should take part in a meeting with the ministers. Parris had managed to delay that meeting, as he wanted to keep his position in Salem Village. But he knew the time had come to say something to the congregation.

In his sermon for the day, Parris noted the divisions in the congregation. He still believed that devils had come to Salem Village. He asked God to forgive him for any mistakes and errors he had made.

He then told the congregation, "I ask that you, too, forgive me for any wrongs I have committed. I tried to do God's will in saving our community, but through ignorance or weakness, I may have been mistaken. It is time for us all to forgive each other."

After the Salem witch trials were ended, even some ministers apologized.

# EPILOGUE

In the years after 1694, more people who had played a role in the Salem witch trials stepped forward to apologize. Among them was Ann Putnam, one of the afflicted girls who had accused many people of being witches. In 1706, when she became a member of the Salem Village church, she said she believed she had falsely accused innocent people. Her actions, she knew, had led to the deaths of Rebecca Nurse and others. All told, 19 people had been hanged as witches. Several more died in jail, and Giles Corey was pressed to death.

Meanwhile, families of some of the people found guilty of witchcraft sought to clear their relatives' names. They presented petitions to the General Court asking to have the verdicts reversed. Other relatives, such as the family of Rebecca Nurse, sought money from the colonial government to pay for legal fees. Salem officials seized the property of others who had been unjustly found guilty of being witches. In 1711 the colonial government agreed to declare many of the accused innocent and pay their families money.

Before that, in 1700, one of the first negative books about the witch trials had been published. In his *More Wonders of the Invisible World*, Robert Calef had particularly harsh words for Cotton Mather. He believed that Mather had been too quick to accept spectral evidence to convict accused witches. Calef thought this even though Mather did at times criticize spectral evidence. Calef thought the accusers were liars and some were trying to hurt neighbors they disliked. He also blamed Salem officials for accepting the accusations without proper evidence.

By the early 1700s more ministers were speaking out against what happened in Salem and the search for witches elsewhere. Educated people began to reject the idea of witchcraft. They thought the signs of affliction some people suffered could be explained by science. The writers on the subject rejected spectral evidence as well. The last recorded witch trial in the American colonies took place

*The Crucible* was staged in China in 2015.

in 1730 in Virginia. As of 1735, witchcraft was no longer a crime in England or its American colonies. By then, more people saw belief in witchcraft as a superstition with no basis in fact.

Over the centuries, people have remained fascinated with the Salem witch hunt. A famous 20th century play about it, *The Crucible*, is still performed around the world. Tourists come to Salem to visit sites connected to the trial.

SALEM WITCH MUSEUM

Historians still disagree on what exactly caused the Salem witch trials. The strong religious beliefs of the Puritans of Salem played a part. So did divisions in the community and fears of the wars on the frontier. Some of the afflicted people may have been suffering from post-traumatic stress

disorder (PTSD). People who take part in wars or experience other forms of violence can develop PTSD, which then creates emotional problems. People like Mercy Lewis, who saw her parents killed, may have suffered from PTSD.

Some scholars have suggested that once the accusations started, more girls and young women accused others of witchcraft because they wanted attention. In a society dominated by men, these girls and women had power for the first time.

Whatever led to the accusations and the trials, the events in Salem remain an important part of American history. The witch trials show the dangers of letting strong beliefs and fears outweigh reasonable thinking, especially when people's lives are at stake.

# TIMELINE

**1689** Samuel Parris becomes minister of the church in Salem Village.

**JANUARY 1692** Betty Parris and Abigail Williams begin to act strangely, and Samuel Parris and others think they are the victims of witchcraft.

**FEBRUARY 1692** Tituba and John Indian, enslaved people working for the Parris family, make a witch cake to try to learn the identity of the witches torturing the girls.

**MARCH 1692** Tituba, Sarah Good, and Sarah Osborne are the first people officially accused of being witches; several more people are accused during the month.

**MAY 1692** George Burroughs, a former minister in Salem Village, is arrested in Maine and brought to Salem on charges that he is a wizard.

**JUNE 1692** Bridget Bishop is the first person found guilty of being a witch and is executed.

**JULY 1692** Massachusetts Bay Governor Sir William Phips decides to pardon Rebecca Nurse, who had been found guilty of witchcraft. He changes his mind after some people in Salem protest. Nurse and four others are hanged on July 19.

**SEPTEMBER 1692** Giles Corey is pressed to death with stones after refusing to enter a plea on the charge of witchcraft.

**OCTOBER 1692** Governor Phips tells officials in England about the witch trials. He orders the trials to stop until he receives word from the king and queen about what to do.

Increase Mather comes out against spectral evidence as proof that someone is a witch or wizard.

**DECEMBER 1692** Cotton Mather publishes his book about the Salem trials and witchcraft, *The Wonders of the Invisible World*.

**JANUARY 1693** Governor Phips frees eight people who had been found guilty of witchcraft.

**MAY 1693** Tituba is released from jail before ever standing trial for being a witch, as the other accused witches are still held in jail.

**NOVEMBER 1694** Samuel Parris delivers a sermon asking forgiveness for his role in the witch scare.

**1706** Ann Putnam, one of the girls who had accused others of being witches, apologizes for her role in sending innocent people to the gallows.

**1730** The last recorded witch trial in colonial America takes place in Virginia.

# GLOSSARY

**afflicted** (uh-FLICK-ted)—suffering from the effects of witchcraft

**allied** (AL-lyd)—people, groups, or countries that work together for a common cause; allies

**communion** (kuh-MYUN-nyen)—Christian rite that honors Jesus' Last Supper, with clergy serving bread and wine

**conjurer** (KON-jer-er)—one who practices magic arts

**congregation** (KON-gri-ga-shen)—people who meet for religious worship

**constable** (KON-stuh-buhl)—a law enforcement official in colonial New England

**deposition** (de-pe-ZI-shen)—testifying, especially before a court of law

**gallows** (GAL-ohz)—a wooden frame used for hanging people convicted of a crime

**magistrate** (ma-jih-STRAIT)—legal and government officials in colonial New England

**parsonage** (PAR-se-nij)—the home where a minister lives

**possessed** (puh-ZEST)—under the spell of a witch or devil

**specter** (SPEK-tur)—a ghost-like image of a real person that can appear far away from the actual person

**spit** (SPIT)—a metal rod that holds meat while it is roasted over an open fire

**tormented** (TOR-ment-id)—made to suffer

# CRITICAL THINKING QUESTIONS

1. According to the Puritans of Massachusetts, why did Satan tempt some people to become witches?

2. How did the warfare in Maine and other parts of New England affect the people of Salem?

3. Why do you think the government of Massachusetts Bay agreed to pay money to some of the relatives of people killed for being witches?

# INTERNET SITES

Use FactHound to find Internet sites related to this book.

Visit *www.facthound.com*

Just type in 9781543541977 and go.

# FURTHER READING

Abrams, Dennis. *Cotton Mather: Puritan Leader.* New York: Chelsea House, 2013.

Gilman, Sarah. *The Salem Witch Trials.* New York: Enslow Publishing, 2017.

Schanzer, Rosalyn. *Witches!: The Absolutely True Tale of Disaster in Salem.* Washington, D.C.: National Geographic Kids, 2017.

Smith-Llera, Danielle. *Exploring the Massachusetts Colony.* North Mankato, MN: Capstone Press, 2017.

# SELECTED BIBLIOGRAPHY

Baker, Emerson W. *A. Storm of Witchcraft. The Salem Trials and the American Experience*. New York: Oxford University Press, 2015.

Boyer, Paul, and Stephen Nissenbaum. *Salem-Village Witchcraft: A Documentary Record of Local Conflict in Colonial New England*. Reprint. Boston: Northeastern University Press, 2016.

Burr, George Lincoln, ed. *Narratives of the Witchcraft Cases, 1648–1706*. New York: Charles Scribner's Sons, 1914. Available online at https://archive. org/stream/narrativeswitch03burrgoog/narrativeswitch03burrgoog_djvu.txt

History of the Salem Witch Trials, http://historyofmassachusetts.org/the-salem-witch-trials/

LaPlante, Eve. *Salem Witch Judge: The Life and Repentance of Samuel Sewall*. New York: HarperOne, 2007.

Norton, Mary Beth. *In the Devil's Snare: The Salem Witchcraft Crisis of 1692*. New York, Knopf, 2002.

Roach, Marilynne K. *The Salem Witch Trials: A Day-by-Day Chronicle of a Community Under Siege*. Lanham, MD: Taylor Trade Publishing, 2004.

Rosenthal, Bernard, general ed. *Records of the Salem Witch-Hunt*. New York: Cambridge University Press, 2009.

Salem Witchcraft Trials, http://famous-trials.com/salem

Salem Witch Trials, http://salem.lib.virginia.edu/home.html

Upham, Charles Wentworth. *Salem Witchcraft; with an Account of Salem Village, and a History of Opinions on Witchcraft and Kindred Subjects*. Vols. I and II. Boston: Wiggin and Lunt, 1867. Available online at https://books. google.com/books?id=7ywLAAAAYAAJ&pg=PR1&source=gbs_selected_pages&cad=3#v=onepage&q&f=false

All Internest sites accessed August 10, 2018.

# INDEX

# ABOUT THE AUTHOR

Michael Burgan is a freelance writer who specializes in books for children and young adults, both fiction and nonfiction. A graduate of the University of Connecticut with a degree in history, Burgan is also a produced playwright and the editor of *The Biographer's Craft,* the newsletter for Biographers International Organization. He lives in Santa Fe, New Mexico.